THE
Archive Photographs
SERIES

KNOWLE
AND
TOTTERDOWN

The blacksmith's shop – thought to have been situated on Redcatch Road.

THE
Archive Photographs
SERIES

KNOWLE
AND
TOTTERDOWN

Compiled by
Mike Hooper, Malcolm Weeks,
Gill Pritchard, Ron Elson,
Tim Treml and Edith Roberts

CHALFORD

First published 1996
Copyright © Mike Hooper, Malcolm Weeks, Gill Pritchard,
Ron Elson, Tim Treml and Edith Roberts, 1996

The Chalford Publishing Company
St Mary's Mill, Chalford,
Stroud, Gloucestershire, GL6 8NX

ISBN 0 7524 0686 8

Typesetting and origination by
The Chalford Publishing Company
Printed in Great Britain by
Redwood Books, Trowbridge

Front cover illustration
The Knowle Anthropological Society, 1897

Also published in the *Archive Photographs* series:
Bishopsworth, Withywood and Hartcliffe
(Anton Bantock and the Malago Society)
Brislington (Mary A. Mitchell, Judith Chard and Jonathan Rowe)

An aerial view of Totterdown and Knowle (to the right). The pattern of tightly packed houses on Pylle Hill is easily identified on any aerial photograph of Totterdown.

Contents

Acknowledgements

We would like to thank the following for their help with supplying photographs and information for this book:

The University of Bath, Bristol Record Office, Somerset Record Office, Wiltshire Record Office, Bristol Reference Library, Bristol City Council Housing Services, Courages Brewery, CSB Garages, The Sisters of Charity, Mr Beacham, Mr Beaven, Mr Bennett, Mervyn Bevan, Mr Chamberlain, Mrs Clark, Pete Clements, Mr Cox, Mrs Elson, Mrs Guy, Mrs Hawker, Mr Keen, Mr and Mrs Keevil, Roger Luker, Miss Merchant, Mr and Mrs Miller, Mr and Mrs Moody, Mike Nelmes, Mr Organ, Mr Parker, Mrs Pearce, Shirley Reinge, Margaret Scott, Doug Semple, Mrs Stevens, Mike Tozer, Mr and Mrs H. Weeks, Mrs P. Weeks, Jennifer Weeks.

Introduction

The names Knowle and Totterdown both give clear indications of their geographical origins. 'Knowle' derives from 'knoll' and means an isolated hill e.g. Brent Knoll in Somerset. Totterdown – a name derived from 'a lookout hill' – also suggests a high area of land.

Evidence of early settlement, particularly in the Knowle West area, was unearthed in 1982, during site levelling for playing fields. This was the former site of Filwood Farm, adjacent to Whitchurch airport. A large amount of pottery and other finds indicated the presence of a Romano-British farming settlement of the second to fourth centuries AD.

The earliest written mention of Knowle (or 'Cnolle' and 'Canolle' as it was variously spelt) appears in the Domesday Book of 1086. It is entered as a manor in its own right – not very large, but important enough to deserve a mention. The Domesday Book states that the land was previously owned by 'Alnoth the Constable' – a man who was later killed in a fight with King Harold's sons, and who was an ancestor of the Berkeley family.

Totterdown is not mentioned in the Domesday Book, but does have a mention in a charter of 1189, under the name of 'Aldebury', which has pride of place as one of the oldest documents housed at the Bristol Record Office. It was written for King John (when he was Count of Mortain – Normandy) and mentions 'the spring in the way near Aldebury'. This spring was an important source of clean water for the inhabitants of the Temple area of Bristol and later in 1586, a conduit was built. The conduit still exists, but the water has been redirected into the River Avon since the hillside was cut through for the railway line at the turn of this century. Other springs, such as Rugewell and Ravenswell, which rise on the Knowle hillside, were also piped into Bristol – to Redcliffe and St Augustine's Abbey – from the thirteenth century.

Knowle West is fortunate in having a fragment of a fifteenth-century building still in existence. This is at Inns Court, not far from the Romano-British settlement mentioned earlier. It consists of a two-storey structure – a small tower which formed part of the much larger semi-fortified house of Sir John Inyn.

In the Bristol Record Office are a series of documents relating to ownership of a toft [homestead] and thirty-four acres of land and three and a half acres of meadow in 'Knoll' next to Bedminster. This belonged to John Colchestre, a barber, and was let at fifteen shillings per year.

Knowle and Totterdown continued purely as an agricultural area and this is clearly shown in the earliest map of the district so far located. It is dated 1633 but is a copy of an earlier one of 1612. It clearly shows the then existing roads, including the Bath and Wells Road and a distinct

St John's Lane. It also features the 'olde farm house' and the 'new farm house'. [See section one, Farms and Farming]. It was still known as 'manor' and belonged to Ezekiel Wallis, a rich Bristol merchant, before being sold to the Methuen family of Corsham Court, Wiltshire.

During the Civil War a 'councell of warre' was held 'at Knowle near Bristol' on the 25 July 1643. The site of this meeting is most likely to have been at Pylle Hill, Totterdown, for on the boundary maps of the early eighteenth century a Totterdown castle is mentioned, although no actual building is shown. The castle was probably a sconce – a temporary, fortified, timber structure.

As early as 1744 there was a prison of some sort at Knowle, for when Bristol privateers captured a number of French ships it is reported that their crews were marched to Knowle. It is thought from available documentary evidence that the site was extensive, stretching along the Wells Road from the present Rookery Road to the Broad Walk area.

In 1756, after the outbreak of the Seven Years War, there were 300 prisoners at Knowle; at the end of the war there were as many as 1,700. Tales of poor treatment were rife, but John Wesley, who visited in 1759, found conditions 'acceptable'. Later, the water supply to the prison failed, and this stopped the prison's re-use for prisoners from the American colonies; the Admiralty was forced to build a replacement at Stapleton.

During the early 1700s, turnpikes were erected at the junction of the Wells and Bath Road, at the present location of Totterdown Bridge and at the junction between Wells Road and St John's Lane. The toll charges were very unpopular and three tollgates in our area were removed illegally by rioters in 1749.

Stagecoaches were often attacked by robbers as they slowed down to negotiate the very steep slopes of Pylle Hill. A new, wider road was designed and was built in 1833, which meant the removal of much of the top of Pylle Hill to reduce the gradient. The houses of Brislington Crescent were built alongside and the road was in use until the recent road improvement scheme in the 1980s.

Speculative house building took place in Totterdown from the 1860s, to house workers for the newly built Temple Meads railway station and for other industries in the central Bristol area. As the available land became infilled at Totterdown, the growth of housing gradually spread out through Knowle. With the increase in population came the need for shops, public houses, entertainment, and all the other services and amenities required by developing suburbs.

It came as a very great shock to the long-established community in Totterdown to learn in the late 1960s that its heart was to be ripped out for the now infamous, unbuilt outer circuit ring-road. 'Totterdown' became synonymous with destruction, but, happily, this association is now fading and a new community has risen from the rubble.

This book helps to tell the story not only of slow growth, but also of quick destruction in two of Bristol's southern suburbs.

One

Farms and Farming

Looking at Knowle in the late twentieth century, with its mixture of local authority estates, Edwardian villas and row upon row of terraced housing, it is difficult to imagine that within living memory there were green fields and farms in parts of the area: cattle were driven along St John's Lane to the market by the Feeder, local milk, cheese and butter were on sale, and fields of barley, potatoes and root crops lay alongside pasture and meadow. Two hundred years ago, the area was completely rural; from Totterdown to Red Lion Hill, from the top of Talbot Road to the Malago were several farming communities going about their daily lives within easy walking distance of Bedminster and Bristol. The land would not have been easy to farm – the countryside is undulating and in places steeply sloped with few fields that could be called truly flat. Unfortunately, the photographic record of this side of Knowle's rural heritage is extremely sparse and the local historian has to rely extensively on documentary evidence from record offices and public libraries.

The earliest record is contained in the Domesday Book of 1086. Knowle ('Canole') was considered important enough to have its own separate entry, distinct from Bedminster with which it is always linked. The survey tells us:

The manor is held by Osbern Giffard. It consists of about 360 acres, one third of which is cultivated for the lord of the manor. The rest is occupied and worked by five villeins [the craftsmen and 'agricultural labourers' of the medieval period] and six cottagers (even more lowly than the villeins). The majority of the land is arable but 16 acres are set aside as meadow, for mowing in summer. The common pasture for grazing is 20 acres and there are about 37 acres of woodland. On the manor there are 8 cattle, 25 pigs and one cob (riding horse). The manor is valued at 40 shillings and has a population of about fifty.

The large open fields of arable land would have been divided into furlongs, which were themselves divided into strips and plots. Each villein would have farmed several strips in each furlong. This arrangement continued until enclosure produced the patchwork of smaller fields so common in the English countryside today. Even so, there were still examples of field strips in the Victoria Park area of Knowle until well into the nineteenth century.

Two hundred years ago, the farming economy of Knowle seems to have been based almost entirely on dairy cattle as described in a book on agriculture written in 1795: 'In the vicinity of Bristol and Bath the scythe is in constant use, and nothing is scarcely seen but the milking pail. Many dairy farmers make butter and half-skimmed cheese and the annual produce per cow is from 8 to 12 pounds'. This description is supported by field names: Greenhills, Clover Paddock, French Grass Ground and Summer Leaze, which all suggest land for grazing, while in such fields as Lilly Mead and Fishers Mead countryfolk would have been seen harvesting the hay. This would have been used not only for winter feed but also to make hay tea – 'The drink is so extremely nutritive that it nourishes the cattle astonishingly. The cattle and horses do not seem to like it at first, but if they are kept till they are very thirsty, they will drink freely of it ever afterwards'.

Work on the farms was hard; agricultural labourers toiled from six in the morning until six in the evening during summer, and in winter from daylight until dark. The rate of wages during harvest time was about nine shillings per week, with dinner and beer; at other times of the year the men were paid seven shillings, with free beer or cider thrown in.

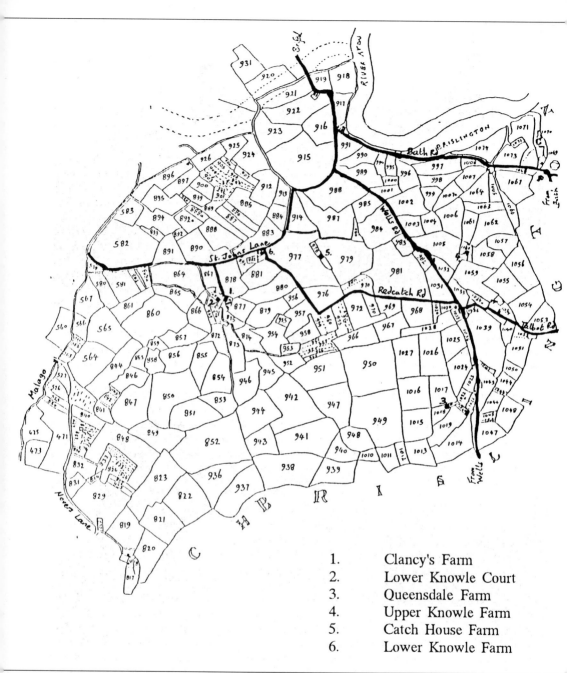

1.	Clancy's Farm
2.	Lower Knowle Court
3.	Queensdale Farm
4.	Upper Knowle Farm
5.	Catch House Farm
6.	Lower Knowle Farm

Knowle farms, as shown on the 1789 map of the manor of Bedminster. By 1605, Knowle was very much a part of the Manor of Bedminster as purchased from Sir Henry Nevill by Sir Hugh Smyth of Ashton Court. Yet a 1612 map still refers to the Manor of Knowle and shows two main farms: the 'ould' in Lower Knowle and the 'new' in Upper Knowle. In 1730, a survey was made of all 'manors', including Bedminster, belonging to the Smyth family. Half a century later, in 1789, in the same book, a further survey was made and for this a contemporary map survives. This evidence, along with the Terrier [inventory] of the Parish of Bedminster compiled in 1826 and the tithe map and award of 1841, shows that there were six main farms in the Knowle area.

Close to St John's Lane, near the junction with Wedmore Vale, were two farmhouses both called 'Lower Knowl Farm'. One farmhouse still exists today. It stands at the end of Berrow Walk and is usually named 'Clancy's Farm' after the last tenant farmer, Michael Daniel Clancy, an Irish cattle dealer. It worked 249 acres of land and its fields lay in the area of Knowle West, centred on Melvin Square. In 1767, the farm was part of the settlement upon the marriage of Sir Jarrit Smith's second son, Thomas.

The second farmhouse was almost adjacent to Clancy's, which can be seen in the background to the left, and was separated from it by a lane. Its site is now occupied by Blagdon Close sheltered accommodation. It was clearly a substantial building; William Bullock, in his will dated 26 April 1674, described it as his 'Mansion House in Lower Knowle'. The building has been identified as Lower Knowle Court in three paintings at Somerset County Archives, one of which can be seen above; an early eighteenth-century map also shows what might be a moated site. In the 1920s the 'moat' was just a pond with a central island where young children would play. This 119-acre farm covered the Marksbury Road/South Bristol College area and stretched as far as Novers Common. Both this farm and Clancy's had the benefit of south-westerly-facing slopes and enjoyed a good water supply from streams and springs.

Queensdale farmhouse was built where Kingshill Road now stands, but there is no evidence for a house upon that site until 1730. This drawing by Samuel Loxton shows the farmhouse in 1919, when it was owned by Mrs Elizabeth Gay, dairywoman. The farm occupied an area of 286 acres and was the largest in Knowle. The fields covered three main parts of the area: Pylle Hill and the ground between St John's Lane and Windmill Hill, Knowle Park, and sections of Upper Knowle. In 1655, two fields called Windmill Closes were let by Robert Paradine, gent to John Goare of Bristol, butcher. The fields are so named on a map of 1677 and provide some evidence of milling – in this case probably of cattle feed – in the Knowle area. Today, the land where the windmill stood lies in the School Road area of Totterdown. Another windmill stood on Windmill Hill close to the farms at Lower Knowle but under independent ownership.

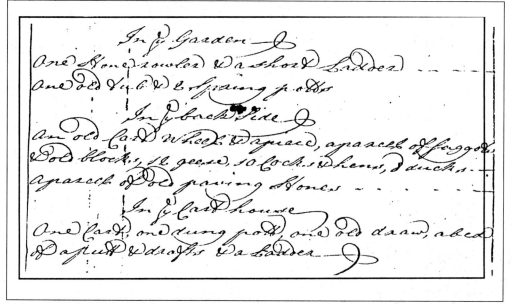

Upper Knowle farmhouse was situated on the north-west junction of Beaconsfield Road and Harrowdene Road but regrettably no pictorial record exists. This was the 'new' farmhouse of the 1612 estate map and it was described in a covenant of 1632 as a 'mansion house'. That it was a substantial building can be ascertained from an inventory drawn up during the time of Edward Buckler, its owner from 1729 until his death in 1739. Buckler was a maltster in Temple Street, 'a great dealer in the malting trade and the sizable owner of a considerable real and personal estate'. Unfortunately, he became a bankrupt 'having frequent occasion for money and being unable to repay his creditors'. Buckler borrowed money from those he had 'worked himself into the good opinion of', putting his farm up as security.

The inventory gives details of the rooms and outbuildings of the farmhouse and their contents, including tools and other artefacts of a farmer's work:

In ye Passage	An old Side Saddle, a bill hook
In ye Millhouse	A Sydermill, a cheese press
In ye Back Side	12 geese, 10 cocks & hens, 8 ducks
In ye Carthouse	One Cart, one dung pott

The presence of a cider mill is a reminder of a popular cottage industry which in this instance may have had an outlet in 'a house called the Green Dragon' which was situated along the turnpike road from Bristol to Wells in a field called Lime Kiln Paddock. Hopefully, the quality was better than that sampled by Celia Fiennes who, in her journal of 1685, declared that the 'natives of Somerset are careless when they made cyder'. The land belonging to Upper Knowle Farm covered 65 acres between the Bath Road and Wells Road. Near the site of The George public house was a limekiln, one of several in Knowle. Lime and refuse coal were burnt to make fertilizer in order to correct the acidity of the soil. On the opposite side of the Wells Road was a small field called Coalpitt Close. Could poor quality coal have been brought there and stored for use in lime burning? Coal-mining was taking place in both Bedminster and Brislington during the eighteenth and nineteenth centuries. One kiln was said to produce enough lime to manure three acres per week. Many farmers still used dung, which they dispersed from dung-pots hanging either side of a horse's saddle. The agriculturalist writing in 1795 stated that 'the operation of 30 cart-loads of dung per acre, after the land has been once limed, has a sensible effect'.

13

FOXWELLS COTTAGE.
UPPER KNOWLE.

Foxwell's cottage was part of the Upper Knowle Farm estate until its demolition *c.* 1896. It stood near the corner of what is now Beaconsfield Road but which used to be a track known as Knowle Farm Road. Records show that a cottage had occupied the site since at least 1720 when the farm belonged to Matthew Walsborough. It is described in an indenture dated 20 June 1720 as 'that new erected messuage and stable lately erected on Lime Kiln Paddock'. Was this the cottage which became known as The Green Dragon where exhausted labourers slaked their thirst on home-made scrumpy?

The cottages' more recent name came from the last tenant of the farm: Thomas Dorney Foxwell, who lived at the farm for over thirty years during the later part of the nineteenth century, and who was described as a farmer and coal-merchant. It was during his tenancy that Upper Knowle Farm became known as Gough Farm – it is so named on the Ordnance Survey map of 1884, though the reason for this is unclear. In *Kelly's Directory* of 1889 it had become Gough Hall Farm and on the 1891 census it was given the grand title of Knowle Manor Farm, perhaps recalling its greater days as the 'new' mansion house of the Manor of Knowle.

During the first half of the nineteenth century, the northern part of the estate was gradually sold off to the Bristol Cemetery Company for the establishment of Arno's Vale Cemetery. By 1902, much of the housing on the north-eastern fringes of Wells Road had been built and soon after that the farm was completely obliterated save for a small copse at the end of Somerset Road. This copse, part of which still remains, was shown on the 1612 map as Seaburn Coppice.

In the area of Perrett's Park, between Redcatch Road and Wells Road, lay the 80 acres of Catch House Farm. The farmhouse stood at the top of Ravenhill Road and can be seen to the left on this 1926 photograph, with Sylvia Avenue running across the foreground. In May 1934, the farmhouse was demolished for make way for housing. During the eighteenth century, the farm belonged to the Elton family. A stream ran through the farm, rising in a field called Raven Hill close to where the park fountain now stands, flowing down to St John's Lane, skirting Pylle Hill and eventually joining the River Avon near its junction with the Feeder.

Catch House Farm from the south-west. In the background are the houses of Knowle Road.

This set of farm buildings at the lower end of Sylvia Avenue was built after the turn of the nineteenth century and survived until the 1930s. In the background can be seen the council houses on Redcatch Road and the Victorian terraces of St John's Lane. A more important group of earlier buildings existed to the south-west, where Redcatch Road meets St John's Lane. This is the site of the 'ould' farmhouse of the Manor of Knowle and it was another known as Lower Knowle Farm. During the eighteenth century, this, too, was under the ownership of the Elton family and the land covered 90 acres, stretching from the Daventry Road area to Redcatch Park. One of the fields was called Lockenwelle – 'a close of pasture ground with a gulley near the middle thereof'. This well or spring was situated behind where the church of St Barnabas now stands and was near the source of the Redcliffe -pipe which carried water from the slopes of Knowle to St Mary Redcliffe.

The farmhouse is referred to in an indenture of bargain and sale, dated 10 May 1629, as 'the Ancient Mannor House (of the Mannor of Knowle) called Lower Knowle Farme'. On the same day, another indenture was drawn up and this mentions 'the late dissolved free Chappell of Knowle late founded in the said Mannor of Knowle'. The survey of 1789 describes the site as 'Lower Knowle House, Garden and Chapel Yard'. From this evidence, it appears that not only is this the site of the most important farm in the area but possibly also that of Knowle chapel which is mentioned in Collinson's *History of Somerset*. The Manor of Knowle eventually came into the possession of the Methuen family of Corsham Court and it is the Methuen archives, kept at the Wiltshire Record Office in Trowbridge, which have yielded most of this information about the farms of Knowle.

16

Two
The Bath Road

This is the Hanham to Knowle tram at Temple Gate in the mid-1930s. The advertisement on the side is for Shepherd's Drapery Store at West Street, Old Market. It is summertime so the driver and conductor are wearing their white cap covers. PC George Jane 58 'B' of the Bristol City Police is on point duty. The buildings in the background have long disappeared – this part of the road being known as Bath Parade. The partially visible building was Usher's Brewery Midland and Great Western Hotel. George's Terminus Commercial Hotel can be seen more fully. Next was Victor Latty's chemist and then Crompton Parkinson's electric-lamp manufacturers.

The Hotwells tram running down the Bath Road with work on the railway embankment taking place, 1932. Note, to the right, the tower of Temple Meads station which was destroyed in the Second World War.

The 1932 embankment work, showing the junctions of the line on the left, running into Temple Meads station and to the right running into St Philip's Marsh.

An aerial view of Pylle Hill depot – part of the Temple Meads complex, with a railway turntable clearly visible – and the near-by Avonclift House, a one-time stay factory.

The Three Lamps signpost dated 1833 in its original position at the junction of the Wells and Bath roads, before the addition of the goldfish bowls. The drinking fountain for man and dog is alongside. The corner shop was Reinge the tobacconist.

Picture of Reinge Brothers on one of their summer outings.

A horse-drawn tram at the Three Lamps Junction, at the turn of the century, shortly before the electrification of the trams. The shop, A.W. Bover, hosier and gents' outfitter, stands in front of Avon Cottage and behind the horses. Next-door is Jacob Wisswasser, the hairdresser. In the background, above the Lavertons Ltd advertisement, can be seen the chimneys of Avon Clift House, once Langridges Stay Manufactory. Next to it, hidden by the tree, are Avon and Bath villas. In 1901, Avon Villa was occupied by Mr and Mrs Parry, who ran the Higher Grade School for boys and girls.

Avon Villa to the left and Bath Villa to the right, 1969. Avon Cottage can be seen, shortly before its demolition.

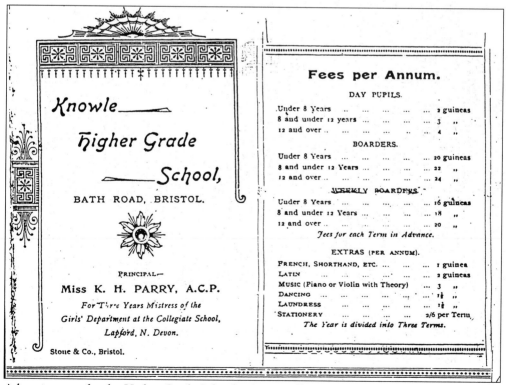

Knowle

Higher Grade

School,

BATH ROAD, BRISTOL.

PRINCIPAL—

Miss K. H. PARRY, A.C.P.

For Three Years Mistress of the
Girls' Department at the Collegiate School,
Lapford, N. Devon.

Stone & Co., Bristol.

Fees per Annum.

DAY PUPILS.

Under 8 Years	2 guineas
8 and under 12 years	3 "
12 and over	4 "

BOARDERS.

Under 8 Years	20 guineas
8 and under 12 Years	22 "
12 and over	24 "

WEEKLY BOARDERS.

Under 8 Years	16 guineas
8 and under 12 Years	18 "
12 and over	20 "

Fees for each Term in Advance.

EXTRAS (PER ANNUM).

FRENCH, SHORTHAND, ETC.	1 guinea
LATIN	2 guineas
MUSIC (Piano or Violin with Theory)	3 "
DANCING	1½ "
LAUNDRESS	1½ "
STATIONERY	2/6 per Term

The Year is divided into Three Terms.

Advertisement for the Higher Grade School – Avon Villa.

Avon Villa and Bath Villa in an advanced state of decay, c. 1972. The picture shows the demolition of all the shops, as well as Avon Cottage and Heber House.

Charles Smith the undertakers, on the Bath Road, January 1966. The lane on the left is May Walk leading to St Philip's and the Bristol Dogs' Home.

Bath Road, looking out of town towards the slopes of Upper Street, Totterdown. On the left is Glanfield Lawrence, the Three-wheeler Car Centre. All of this was removed for the road widening scheme. All the properties, up to The Turnpike Inn, have been demolished.

Brislington Crescent, 1970. This was built after the Bath Road was widened in 1833.

Looking back towards the Three Lamps junction from Upper Street. On the right can be seen the partly cleared Brislington Crescent; between these houses and the river, on the extreme right, lies the original turnpike road to Bath. In the immediate foreground, on the left, is County Street, followed by Angers Road and New Walls Road.

Just beyond Totterdown Bridge was the boat-yard of R.T. Brown and Sons Ltd – Lighterage. The back of the very tall houses on the Bath Road can be seen.

Advertisement for the Bristol Tramway and Carriage Co. Ltd. The tramway from Bristol Bridge to Totterdown was sanctioned in February 1876.

One of the most spectacular monuments in Bristol General Cemetery (popularly known as Arno's Vale Cemetery) is that of Raja Rammohan Roy, a founder of the Indian Independence Movement, who died on a visit to the city in 1833 and was later reburied here. This picture was taken on 11 November 1923.

Arno's Vale Cemetery, looking towards Somerset Road. The tram could be taken to the Totterdown terminus and from here it was a few minutes walk to the cemetery. The cemetery cost £16,837 to build and was consecrated in October 1840.

Three
The Wells Road, Totterdown

As Totterdown and then parts of Knowle started to become urbanised during the nineteenth century, the increase in population brought with it a need for establishments where people could buy the goods and find the services they required, rather than travel into Bristol or Bedminster. Starting around 1870, short terraces of shops began to appear along the Wells Road so that by the early 1900s the stretch from The Three Lamps to Broad Walk had a wide selection of emporia interspersed with private housing. Just as today we can satisfy most of our shopping needs in a large supermarket, so the residents of Victorian Totterdown and Knowle had the full range of shopping facilities within easy reach of home. Shoppers within Wells Road will have seen many changes; while some establishments purveyed the same type of goods for many years, some premises changed hands and the nature of business frequently, and others reverted to domestic use. In this chapter, we shall 'wander' up Wells Road as far as Knowle Road looking at some shops and other premises which flourished until wholesale demolition for a new road system almost totally devastated the area in 1972.

The 2 Ways Café at the Three Lamps junction.

A photograph of J.S. Garlick.

John Stanley Garlick, at Nos 22-24 Wells Road, newsagent and stationer, 1912, with billboards galore proclaiming a host of different news stories: 'Titanic Enquiry Resumes' (*Daily Press*), 'Dock Strikes' (*Daily Herald* – the Labour newspaper – and the *Daily Chronicle*), 'Derby Probables' (*Sporting Life*). The shop also offered a GWR parcels service. On either side of Garlick's were S.G. Hutchings, picture-frame-makers (No. 20) and T.R. Cox, boot and shoemakers (No. 26).

H.S. Jones, upholsterer, occupied No. 12, which boasted a fine door in the art nouveau style. The shop-front has been built out from the original house. At No. 12a cats and dogs could be pampered at the Three Lamps Canine and Feline Beauty Parlour.

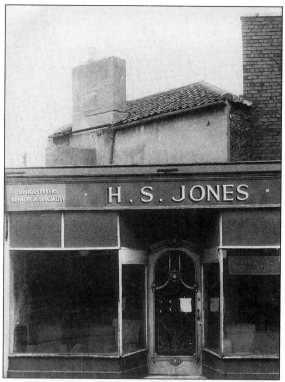

Further up towards New Walls Road we see a group of premises ready for demolition. From the left: Telecraft, TV repairs (No. 56); Archibald Wallace Wilson and Son, hairdressers (No. 58); Lahore Café and Club (No. 60): Brooks' Cleaners (No. 26).

Nos 28-66 Wells Road were originally known as Totterdown Terrace (Nos 1-20) and the last two premises in the row, on the corner of New Walls Road, were occupied by Jonathan Fanson and Co., hardwaremen. Established in 1871 as Joseph Fanson, carpenter and blind-maker, the firm sold a wide variety of products: brooms, buckets and hurricane lamps were displayed outside the shop, oil and turpentine were dispensed inside. This photograph, dating from about 1897 shows that the premises had three storeys.

By the 1930s No. 66 had lost its top storey and the two shops offered different services: china and glass (No. 64) and ironmongery (No. 66). Next-door was Brooks' dyers and drycleaners.

The Home and Colonial Stores Ltd, provision merchants, which had stood on the corner of Angers Road from the very early years of this century. It is showing off its well-turned-out staff and manager. This was one of the first 'chain-stores', with branches all over Bristol and in other large towns and cities.

Part of the row of shops above Angers Road, late 1960s. No. 90 was Rollo's ladies outfitter, which stood opposite St John's Lane. Between the first floor windows is a Bedminster boundary stone.

The sad sight of shops closed prior to the demolition in 1972, looking down Wells Road towards The Three Lamps from just above Angers Road. On the right from the foreground are Blake's Bakeries Ltd (Nos 86-88); Maynards, confectioners (No. 84); Home and Colonial (No. 80); Boots, the chemist (No. 78), H.W. Stevens, draper (No. 76), H. Playfair Ltd, boot manufacturers (No. 74).

Crossing over the Wells Road to the Totterdown Linen Warehouse, the emporium of John William Way, draper, milliner and house-furnisher. This shop between Cheapside Street and Bush Street occupied Nos 77-81. This 1905 photograph shows that one of John Way's specialities was CB corsets. Later the business moved to No 341 Wells Road.

Looking back from Bushey Park, *c.* 1903. Tram 87 is en route to Bristol Bridge. A horse-drawn cart can be seen, as well as a brewer's dray outside the Phoenix Hotel. The shops on the right are part of the row between Angers Road and County Street, known as County Place. They include: William Goodall, bootmaker (No. 96); Henry Hodder and Co., chemists and druggist (No. 94); Frederick William Blythe, post office, stationer and photographer (No. 92); Arthur J. Sims, grocer (No. 90). On the left, after The Phoenix and W.J. Way we can see Samuel Thomas Pont, grocer (No. 75) and the Maypole Dairy (No. 73A).

A later photograph of the same view, taken in 1966. Cars are queuing down Wells Road. Nearly all the shops have changed hands many times; England's Smart Shoes are at No. 96; Hodder's (No. 94); Shepherd's stationers (No. 92). Across the road: McClary Easy Self-Service Laundry (No. 83); A. Duggan, turf accountant (No. 81); Cranbrook Radios, radio and television dealers (No. 79), Speedy Shoe Services (No. 77).

Bush Street linked Wells Road with Oxford Street, with St John's Lane angling off to the south-west. On the corner is the Phoenix Hotel. On the opposite corner The Midland Bank is 'no longer listening'. Along the left side of Bush Street are: W. Bennett, greengrocer (No. 3); A.E. Chidley, confectioner (No. 5); Cyril Slater, bacon curer (Nos 7-7a). Two shops can be seen in Oxford Street; B.J. Mildred, turf accountant (No. 117), who has moved from a demolished Wells Road property, and Totterdown sub-post office (No. 118).

Showing off the delivery van for Keen's Electric Bakery – complete with telephone number. This site has had at least a hundred years use as a bakery; before Keen, the baker was Joseph Smith and before him John Lowe.

The site between Bushy Park and St John's Lane is shown occupied by the Westminster Bank and The Bush Hotel. Totterdown Hotel stands opposite.

Above Bushy Park in this 1959 view we can see Totterdown YMCA (Nos 101-107, including at No. 105, Lloyds Bank); Knowle Picture House (Nos 109-111) then showing *Bobbikins* (the architect was W.H. Watkins, a specialist in cinema design, who also worked on Merrywood grammar school; Fleetway Publications (No. 113) advertising *Women's Weekly*; E. Mitchell, wine and spirit merchants (No. 115); W.F. Pope, motor-car accessories (No. 117).

From Knowle Road many of the shops and premises already mentioned can be seen. No. 2 Knowle Road, on the left, was Dr Joseph Sluglett's surgery, previously Dr David Robertson's.

Looking up the Wells Road from Bushy Park with County Street opposite. Many of the shops are boarded up though most retain some form of identity: Bristol Co-operative Society (Nos 104-106); K.E. Humphries, fishmonger (No. 108); M.R. Stacey, ladies' outfitter (No. 110); David Greig (No. 112); Humphries and Son, butchers (No. 114), later to be found across the road at Nos 147-149; Cadena Café (No. 116); Victoria Wine (No. 118). Crossing Highgrove Street we come to: Parker's bakeries (No. 120); SWEB service centre (No. 122); Bollom's, valet service (No. 124); V. and W. Hutton, florists (Nos 126-128); R.F. Norcott, butcher (No. 130); Paxman's, dyers (No. 132); Padfield's, estate agents (No. 134).

The interior of David Greig, prior to demolition. Note the famous thistle motif – a distinctive feature of the decoration on the walls and counter. Greig's occupied No. 112 Wells Road for fifty years. It was very popular with housewives of Knowle and Totterdown, selling quality goods at reasonable prices.

Four
The Wells Road, Knowle

A view up the Wells Road from the corner of Crowndale Road, *c.* 1915. Tram 211 is climbing Knowle Hill en route from Bristol Bridge towards the terminus at The Red Lion. Standards carrying overhead wires for the trams are interspersed with lamp posts. The line from Bristol Bridge to Totterdown was electrified on 5 December 1900 and from Totterdown to Knowle a fortnight later. On the right can be seen the tall building of Knowle police and fire station. On the left are several shops: Davis and Dart, grocers (No. 194); F.R. Beer, confectioner (No. 196); Richard Henry Brown, pork butcher (No. 198) whose daughter Alice is pictured inset on her Excelsior motor-cycle; Harry Day, fruiterer (No. 200 on the corner of Clyde Road). The latter two shops were previously (1897) private houses. No. 200 has been Wang's Fish and Chip Bar for over thirty years.

Looking back down Wells Road from the corner of Rookery Road. In the distance is Holy Nativity church before the tower was built in 1931. The building was destroyed in 1940 and rebuilt to a different design. On the right, behind the trees is the Baptist chapel. The shops in view are: Davis and Dart, grocers (No. 194), F.R. Beer, confectioner (No. 196).

A modern view shows Holy Nativity with the tower which survived the bombing. All the houses have been converted to shops. A telephone box has been on its site for over eighty years. Private housing was replaced by a motor engineers in 1928 and later by a Texaco service-station.

The grand house on the left (No. 254) was called 'Arcadia' but known locally as 'Lemonade Palace'. It belonged to Charles Edward Beavis, mineral water manufacturer of Jacob Street, Old Market. It is now the premises of Cleve House Day School for Boys and Girls. The houses opposite have yet to be built.

William Spencer Edmonds, stationer and tobacconist, provided many other services, including bookseller, hairdresser and umbrella repair. The display stand to the left of the shop-front was a permanent feature. At Christmas-time it was used to display dolls and toys. The premises (No. 286) now houses part of the National Westminster Bank. The houses beyond were bombed in the Second World War and rebuilt as shops.

The premises of the Union of London and Smith's Bank stood on the corner of Greenmore Road. The man and his dog are suitably posed in this photograph from c. 1910. Greenmore Road was developed and named after two local worthies: Robert Edward Greenhough, a linen draper at the corner of Cheapside Street (1889) and living at No. 236 Wells Road (1906) and Alderman Frank Moore of Knowle House.

Part of Victoria Buildings, No. 302 stood on the corner of Talbot Lane. This 1905 photograph shows E. & F. Baker, butchers, displaying their Christmas wares and advertising 'choice' Southdown sheep, poultry, heifers and venison. The man on the right holds a pole with a hook to reach the higher birds. To the left was Sidney Chard, ironmonger. Up above the present shop-fronts, the original first floors can still be seen.

The group of shops between Greenmore Road and Talbot Lane was known as Victoria Buildings and was established c. 1900. This photograph shows three of the premises: Henry John Savery, confectioner (No. 294), whose private residence was Scropton Lodge, Beaconsfield Road; Edward Rudman, high class family grocer (No. 296), complete with delivery cart; Mrs Jemima Sherbourne, Victoria dairy (No. 298).

Miss Nellie Windmill, who took over No. 298 in 1906 and sold confectionery. In a little room off the shop, customers could sit at tables and partake of delicious ice-creams.

Miss Mabel Windmill, who helped her sister to run the sweet shop, and the girls' father, Herbert Charles Windmill, who was a saddler and in 1887, operated from No. 18 and later from No. 56 Wells Road.

This photograph from *c.* 1950 shows some of the premises between Talbot Lane and Priory Road. A milk cart is passing The Talbot Inn, with the shops of Victoria Buildings beyond. The shops in view are: Henry French, stationer and post office (No. 316); Miss Ada Partridge, draper (No. 318); William Blight, boot and shoe manufacturer (No. 320).

William Arthur Wakefield, confectioner, prior to 1939, after which he moved into Windmill's shop. The premises is now occupied by Bollom's dry-cleaners.

A good view of the old cottages near the corner of Redcatch Lane. This 1905 photograph shows a tram stop opposite the gate of No. 321. Part of Upper Knowle Wesleyan church can be seen.

The cottages were replaced by shops in 1913 and later the premises in Redcatch Lane were extended to fill in the angle on the corner with the Wells Road.

A busy scene showing the shopping area around The Talbot Inn, *c.* 1923. The shops on the right include: Graham H. Smith, ironmonger (No. 319); Allan Ball, chemist (No. 321); Knowle Town sub-post office (No. 323); Knowle Motor Company with premises behind the shops (No. 323a); Robert William Benge, pork butcher (No. 325); E. Luton and Sons, bakers (No. 327); Thomas Gilbert Elliot, butcher (No. 329); Keen's the bakers (No. 331).

This 1987 photograph shows some changes. Nos 319 to 323 remain with new fronts with No. 323 still being the Post Office. The rest of the buildings have been demolished and replaced by modern premises – erected to form part of the Broadwalk Shopping Centre.

Robert William Benge, pork butcher, *c*. 1913. To the left can be seen part of Henry Day's greengrocer's and poulterer's premises. To the right is the lane leading to the backyard!

Here, behind Benge's shop, pigs were fattened before providing bacon and cured ham for discerning customers. The man in apron and boots holds the lethal weapons. The straw was used to burn off the bristles.

Arthur Percival Keen ran a bakers at No. 331. This photograph from *c*. 1920 shows that Hovis is all the rage and upstairs a café offered tea, cakes and sandwiches. The tall property to the left belonged to Henry Mountain.

This view of the Wells Road shows the shops shortly before their demolition in 1972 and replacement by the Broadwalk Shopping Centre.

Smith's the ironmongers of No. 319 had moved by 1933 to become Smith & Co. of No. 343 and had expanded to include workshops at the back on land which stretched to an entrance in Broad Walk. The owner of C.G. Smith was the hon. secretary of Bristol and District Ironmongers Association. This photograph also shows Lloyds Bank, on the left of Smith's.

'May we help you?' at Smith's first shop, with Mr Llewellyn Lewis in the middle and Mr Bottomly on the right.

Photocall for Smith's staff, before a coach outing. Notice the concrete air-raid shelters.

Near the other end of Redcatch Lane is a row of shops just before the junction with Axbridge Road. This 1951 photograph shows the last of the row – Arthur Harold Jones, hardware dealer (No. 249). Many familiar brands are on display: Mazda and Crompton light bulbs, Lux, Tide, Rinso and Dreft washing powders. The young assistant is Dan Jones, son of the owner.

No. 70 at the Red Lion terminus. The display shows route ten – Knowle to Bristol Bridge. All eyes on the camera. The presence of a lady conductor indicates that the photograph almost certainly dates from the years of First World War when for the first time lack of manpower opened up previously male-dominated occupations to women.

A tram about to depart for Bristol Bridge at the Red Lion terminus.

Opposite the Red Lion stood Knowle Terminus Garage. 'The most modern service-station in the suburbs', it replaced private houses c. 1935. This photograph shows the property suitably adorned for the celebration of George VI's coronation. On that day this garage sold the second largest amount of petrol in Bristol. No wonder the proprietor, G. Allan Clark (on the right) looks satisfied. A range of fuels is on sale including Regent Super and Discol. KLG spark plugs are also advertised. The first floor of the premises was used as accommodation by the family.

Blue Star took over the garage in 1962 offering a new battery from 58s 6d and 'nine months to pay on tyres'. By the early 1970s, the sale of petrol 'across the pavement' was forbidden in towns and the garage was later sold to R.W. and P. Dickinson in 1974.

Knowle, Bristol.

Wells Road leaves Knowle and enters Hengrove at Bears Bridge. This photograph, taken early this century, looks back towards Bristol and shows a few houses on the top of Red Lion Hill.

By 1935 this area is becoming more familiar. Airport Road has been constructed to the left and a row of shops has appeared just above the junction: Hector Leadbeater, corn and flour dealer was at No. 463; Benjamin Victor Sunderland, fruiterer (No. 465); Arthur Froggard, tobacconist (No. 467).

Five
Public Houses

In Bristol there were two breweries: Bristol United Brewery, formed in 1889, which occupied a modern brewery (for that time) in Rupert Street and George's of Bath Street (off Victoria Street) now Courage's Brewery.

In the early days, public houses and off-licences tended to remain with the same family over the generations. The emphasis was on the high quality of beer and its price, rather than the comfort of the interior, as is often the case today. Bread, cheese and onions was the food most generally offered. Many of the publicans were individuals with great characters – a dying breed.

The Pylle Hill area of Totterdown appeared to have a pub and an off-licence on every street corner, whilst in Knowle the pubs were much scarcer.

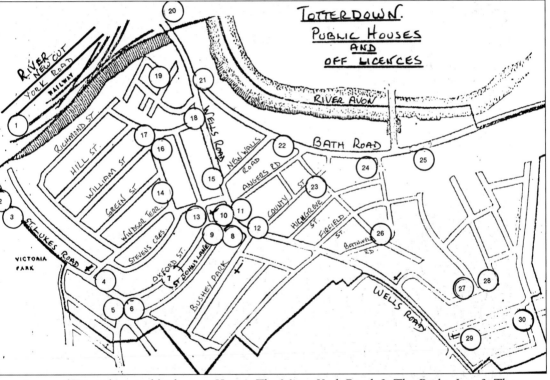

A map of Totterdown public houses. Key: 1. The Mitre, York Road; 2. The Bridge Inn; 3. The Princess Royal; 4. The Cumberland Hotel; 5. The Boar's Head; 6. Three Elms Inn; 7. The Robin Hood; 8. The Bush Hotel; 9. not named, but on the 1882 map; 10. The Phoenix; 11. The Prince Rupert; 12. Totterdown Hotel; 13. The Oxford; 14. The New Found Out (previously The Builders Arms); 15. The Bell; 16. The Shakespeare; 17. The King William; 18. The Raglan; 19. off-licence, Higham Street; 20. Bath Bridge Tavern; 21. Blue Bowl; 22. The Swan; 23. Stanley House off-licence; 24. Turnpike Inn; 25. The Three Lamps; 26. off-licence, top of Summer Hill; 27. off-licence, corner of Park Street and School Road; 28. off-licence, School Road; 29. off-licence, 15 Sydenham Road; 30. off-licence, end of Sydenham Road.

The Mitre situated at No. 164 York Road, between St Luke's Road and Bath Bridge. The proprietor in 1929 was Harry Stevens.

The Bridge Inn, No. 2 St Luke's Road. This was before the widening and deepening of the road under the railway bridge.

The Princess Royal, at the bottom of St Luke's Steps, with Victoria Park in the background.

The Cumberland Hotel on St Luke's Road at the bottom of Windsor Terrace.

Three Elms, No. 77 Oxford Street. This was demolished for the road scheme that was never built. Opposite this pub was The Boar's Head, which later became a double-glazing premises.

The Shakespeare on the corner of Henry Street and William Street. Mrs Morgan ran this pub in the late 1920s. It was another George's outlet. Just across the road was The King William public house, which is now the Glasnost Restaurant.

The New Found Out, Green Street and Henry Street.

The Raglan, on the corner of Wells Road and Cambridge Street. It is under this building that the spring issues, which was piped to the Temple area.

Blue Bowl. This attractive public house was on the Bath Road near the Three Lamps junction.

The Swan was situated on the Bath Road on the corner of Angers Road. It was originally an ordinary house, which had extended in the late nineteenth century to accommodate a bar. It was at one time run by two sisters and was one of only two public houses in Bristol to sell Guinness imported directly from Ireland in boats which docked at Welsh Back.

The Turnpike Inn, near Totterdown Bridge, was built just after the 1833 road improvements. There may have been an earlier building near the site at which the extra horses, required to pull the stage coaches up the steep incline of Pylle Hill, were kept.

Stanley House off-licence, on the corner of Stanley Hill and County Street. This, too, was 'swept away' in the early 1970s for road improvements.

The Phoenix, on the corner of Bush Street and Wells Road.

Totterdown Hotel on the corner of Wells Road and the top of County Street. This picture shows the attractive green-tiled frontage, that was once so common in Bristol.

The Bush Hotel at the top of St John's Lane, on the bend of the Wells Road. The original Bush Hotel was much smaller and was surrounded by a garden so this well-known frontage was a later addition. Note the old-style police box. Sadly, all this was demolished for the road scheme.

The Bell Inn, No. 65 Wells Road, another George's pub, which faced New Walls Road.

The George, Wells Road – during an early refurbishment.

ELIGIBLE OPPORTUNITY FOR INVESTMENT.

TO BE

SOLD BY AUCTION,

By Messrs. RIDDLE & DEW,

AT THE COMMERCIAL ROOMS, IN THE CITY OF BRISTOL,

On WEDNESDAY, October 31st, 1838,

AT ONE O'CLOCK IN THE AFTERNOON,

In the following, or such Lots as may be agreed upon at the time of Sale,

LOT 1.—ALL THAT

FREEHOLD MESSUAGE

Or Dwelling-House,

BEING THE WELL-FREQUENTED

INN or TAVERN, called or known as the GEORGE INN,

With the capital Stables, Outhouses, Skittle Alley, and Bowling Green,

Situate at UPPER KNOWLE, in the Parish of Bedminster, in the County of Somerset, now in the occupation of Mr. John Loader, as Yearly Tenant thereof, at the low rental of £30 per Annum.

An advertisement for The George Inn when it was sold in 1838 for £482.

United Breweries off-licence at the corner of Redcatch Lane and Wells Road, *c.* 1905.

The Talbot, Wells Road.

The Red Lion from a drawing made after refurbishment early this century.

Leinster House, Knowle West in the 1930s.

Six
Church Life

At the time of the Reformation, a small chapel of 'Knowle' is known to have been in existence, whose only possession, it seems, was a chalice weighing only nine ounces. The exact location of this chapel is not known. Between the years 1861 and 1932, as the area developed, sixteen churches and chapels were built, plus the chapel attached to the convent of the Sisters of Charity – an Anglican order of nuns – meeting the needs of the growing population. Some of these people, however, continued to attend churches in the central areas of Bristol from which they had moved. Many of these chapels were nonconformist. Over the years churches have disappeared or merged, suffered at the hands of German bombers, or been redeveloped to meet changing needs.

Exterior of St Luke's church, York Road. Founded in 1861 and built on spoil from the New Cut, it was built to serve the poor in the parish of Bedminster. The first vicar, Rev. David Alfred Doudney, also ran the near-by soup kitchen. The ornate stone parapet to the tower which can be seen in the photograph on page 68, has been removed as it had become a danger to the public.

Interior of St Luke's church, York Road, 1950. Note the overhead gas heaters.

In the centre of this 1926 photograph is St Luke's church, with its tower complete, and to the right is the rose window of Wycliffe Congregational chapel, Windsor Terrace, Totterdown. On the skyline can be seen the newly completed Royal Fort building.

Choir of Wycliffe Congregational chapel, Windsor Terrace, Totterdown.

Carols around the Christmas tree in the Wycliffe Congregational chapel, 1950s.

Girl weds 'the boy next-door'. The wedding of Grace Milton of No. 25 Green Street to Harold Weeks of No. 24 Green Street, at Wycliffe Congregational chapel, on 3 September 1949.

Oxford Street Methodist chapel which was closed on 26 August 1962 after ninety years. It was demolished in the 1970s.

Totterdown Methodist church (Bushey Park), 1925, showing the interior before the alterations.

Bushey Park Wesleyan chapel. This is now known as Totterdown Methodist church.

The scout group celebrating their twenty-first anniversary at Totterdown Methodist church, 1949.

The former Angers Road Methodist church, Totterdown. This was latterly used as a garage.

rom "The Fairy Gifts" play, given by pupils of the Misses Winifred Mobey and Irene Yeomans, Road Methodist Church, Totterdown, Bristol.

A play entitled *The Fairy Gifts* at Angers Road Methodist church.

Vicars attached to the Knowle mission, 1898.

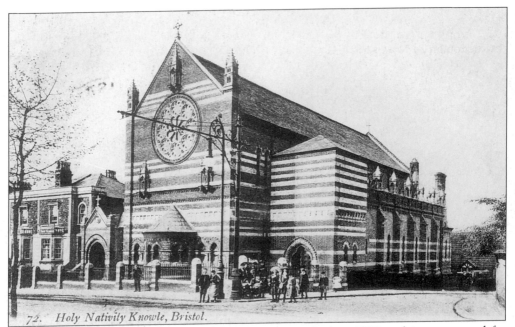

72. *Holy Nativity Knowle, Bristol.*

The church of Holy Nativity. Its foundation stone was laid in 1870 and it was opened for worship in 1871. It was finally consecrated on 4 June 1883 by the bishop of Gloucester. The first vicar was the Rev. Hanbury-Tracy.

Holy Nativity Parochial Hall, Goolden Street. This was used for religious services after the church was 'blitzed' on 24 November 1940. Mr Goolden gave the land for the building of the church. The houses of Garibaldi Terrace in the background were cleared and the children's playground now stands on the site.

The beginning of the re-building of
Holy Nativity church after its
destruction on 24 November 1940.

The commencement of the structural
re-building of Holy Nativity church.
Note the 'Clock Re-building Appeal'.

75

Totterdown Baptist church, on the corner of Sydenham and Cemetery roads.

Knowle Methodist church, formerly Upper Knowle Wesleyan School chapel. Originally it was intended to be the Sunday school.

The Institute garden party on 10 September 1921 at Knowle Wesleyan chapel (now Knowle Methodist church) on the corner of Redcatch Road and the Wells Road.

Upper Knowle Wesleyan School chapel concert group.

The re-opening of Upper Knowle Methodist church on Saturday, 13 June 1951, by one of the original trustees, Mr Charles Austin. On 2 December 1940 a bomb fell outside the cellar door in Redcatch Road, which caused extensive damage to the wall and roof of the church, in addition to weakening the foundations.

Preparations for the demolition of the old school room and the building of a new hall attached to Upper Knowle Methodist church. This was opened on Saturday, 15 September 1979 by the oldest member, Mrs Mable Higginson, who had attended the first Sunday school in 1904. The houses of Oakmeade Park are on the right and Chards Yard can be seen in the background.

Harrowdene Methodist church. Between the wars, Miss Gladys Rowe produced annual children's concerts involving many members of the Sunday school.

Rev. and Mrs Craddock of Harrowdene Methodist church.

Harrowdene Methodist Christmas production of Robin Hood, 1936.

No. 17 Jubilee Road, Knowle, where the congregation of St Gerard Majella Roman Catholic church, Knowle, first met in 1909. The confessional was in a cupboard! Later, this building was the well-known Tozer's Dairy. Tozer's Hill is on the right-hand side of this picture.

St Gerard Majella, at the top of Talbot Hill.

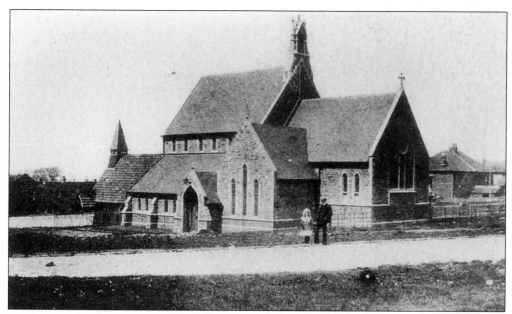

St Martin's, daughter church of Holy Trinity, in its original form at the turn of the century.

St Martin's scout group.

Rev. Gobbitt on his departure from St Martin's in 1942.

The Houses of Charity, Knowle, *c.* 1905 before the completion of the main façade.

Looking down Redcatch Lane showing the construction of the remainder of the façade of the Houses of Charity and also St Elizabeth's Home and St Vincent's Lodge on the right, which is now St Peter's Lodge, Tennis Road. Redcatch Park has since replaced the allotments on the left.

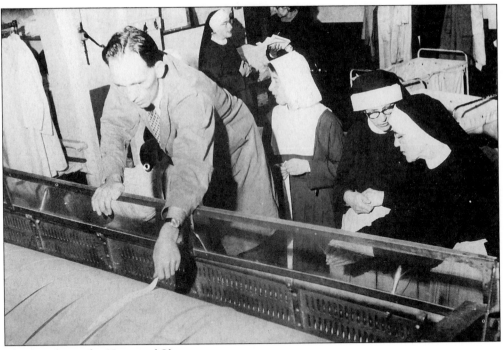

The laundry at the Houses of Charity.

The altar in the chapel in 1994 prior to the sale of the convent.

Seven
School Life

Education in Knowle and Totterdown prior to 1870 and the passage of Forster's Education Act consisted of 'dame' schools, Sunday schools and private schools. The Act made the education of all children compulsory and elected school boards were created to supervise the Act in districts where schools had been built by voluntary effort. The schools in our area were originally part of the Bedminster School Board, but were taken over by the Bristol School Board in 1897 when the city boundary was extended. In 1902, the school boards were abolished and responsibility for education was taken over by the Local Education Authority (LEA).

In addition to the LEA schools there were two main private schools – Charlton House School at No. 230 Wells Road, and the collegiate school on the corner of Priory Road and Wells Road, which later transferred to the premises now occupied by Cleve House School (Arcadia). Another local school of note was Knowle Open Air School opened in 1913 as the first in Bristol.

A girls' class at Knowle Junior School (School Road), late nineteenth century.

Miss Hannah Vimpany's class at Knowle Infants' School 1905-06. Miss Vimpany was headteacher here from 1898 to 1930.

Knowle Junior School in 1936. The headmistress on the left is Miss King. Note in the centre of the front row the girl in the dark gym slip, who was from St Agnes' Home, run by the Sisters of Charity.

One of the Christmas productions performed by Knowle Junior School – *The Wizard who Forgot*, 1948.

Knowle Park Juniors, *c.* 1947.

Knowle Park Juniors' sports day in 1948, held at the Greyhound Stadium.

The presentation by Alderman Chamberlain to Mr Proudlove on his retirement from Knowle Park Junior School in 1957. To the right is Mrs Marjorie Wright (*née* Smith, of the Bath Road funeral directors family), a teacher at the school.

Miss Bale's class at Knowle Park Juniors, 1950s.

Mrs Wright's class, Knowle Park Juniors, 1961. The headmaster, Mr King, is on the left.

Wells Road Infant School on Maxse Road, *c.* 1900. The school was demolished in the blitz of 24 November 1940.

Wells Road Infant School in the mid-1920s, with the headmistress, Miss Hurditch, taking a class in the hall.

Wells Road Senior Girls' School, *c.* 1922.

A flower-growing competition in the hall of Wells Road Junior School, 1932. The headmaster was Mr Foweraker.

Wells Road Senior Boys' School team, winners of the Woodcock Shield for soccer, 1939-40.

Knowle Open Air School in the process of being demolished, 1991. The school was founded in 1913 with voluntary contributions from Miss Townsend, a member of the Bristol School Board. The school was taken over by Bristol Education Committee in 1920. It was built for sick and ailing children who were initially referred by head teachers with the final selection made by the school's medical officer. The school closed in March 1940 and the children transferred to South Bristol Open Air School, Novers Hill.

Eight
Recreation and Leisure

As Totterdown and subsequently Knowle developed, so the opportunities for recreation and leisure increased. Some were of a sedentary nature with cinemas in Totterdown and then Knowle (alas, both no more). There were no local theatres or music halls but a number of local amateur dramatic groups, attached to local churches. The first municipal public library was housed in temporary premises and then the present purpose-built building. Public parks developed in Victorian times with Victoria Park between Totterdown and Windmill Hill, then Perret Park and finally, after the Second World War, the allotments in Redcatch Road were turned into Redcatch Park. Opportunities for the sports spectator varied through time, from the racecourse and speedway stadium to the motor-cycle street races in Totterdown. For those of a more active nature, a number of sports clubs and facilities developed and continue to this day: the golf course, now largely covered by the Knowle Park estate and transferred to the edge of Stockwood; swimming baths – open-air at Victoria Park and covered at Jubilee and, more recently, at Filwood; a rugby field; a cricket ground; tennis-courts; bowling-greens; and an athletics ground. Teams represented all these major sports and a number of rugby and soccer clubs.

Dame Clara Butt, the famous opera singer who lived in Bellevue, Totterdown.

The temporary library in Knowle Road. It operated from October 1922 until March 1938.

The replacement library, opened in 1938 and still in use today. Note the lack of trees at the rear of the library.

The Knowle Picture House on Wells Road. This cinema was opened in 1913.

The construction of the Gaiety Cinema, Knowle in 1933. Both cinemas were owned by the Chamberlain family.

Gaiety Cinema soon after opening, 1934.

Motor-cycle club meeting outside the Gaiety Cinema in the late 1930s.

A mid-1930s aerial view of Knowle Stadium, used for greyhound racing and speedway. The speedway started here on 25 August 1928. Red Lion Hill is to the top and the Imperial Sports Ground to the right.

A crowd at the speedway. The Robbins family of Totterdown are much in evidence supporting the Bristol Bulldogs.

Race underway.

Speedway team with the mascot 'Meg' the dog, loaned for the team photo by Jennifer Pearson, 1948 season.

SPEEDWAY   RIDERS

1951
CHAMPIONSHIP
OF THE WORLD

CHAMPIONSHIP ROUND

BRISTOL

SPEEDWAY

FRIDAY
AUGUST 31ST

ONE SHILLING

Motor-cycle road racing, Vale Street, 1913. Vale Street, Totterdown, was used for testing motor-cycles and cars as it was the steepest urban street in England.

The race-course at Knowle was opened on 19 March 1873 by the Prince of Wales, with an estimated crowd of 100,000 in attendance. However, its popularity was short-lived and it closed, a financial failure, in 1880.

The pavilion at Knowle race-course, which was said to hold 'three thousand people'.

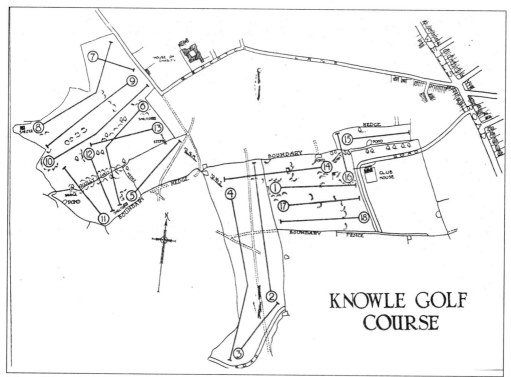

Map of Knowle golf-course, much of which was laid out on the old race-course, around the time of the First World War.

Knowle cricket pavilion, 1905.

Knowle cricket team, 1914 season.

Knowle tennis-courts and bowling-green, with crowds to the left, watching the cricket.

Knowle Tennis Club, 1920s.

Knowle Tennis Club, 1960s. From left to right: Gwyneth Pearce, Cis Wareham, Beryl Combs, Gwen Manning, Eileen Organ and Sheila Rice.

Knowle Ladies hockey team, 1940s.

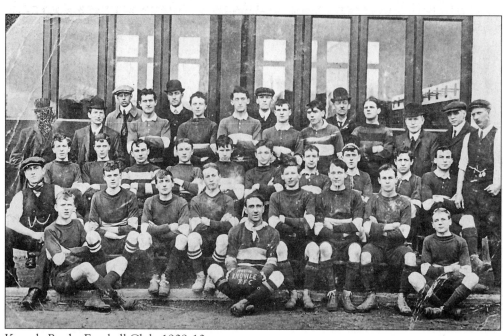

Knowle Rugby Football Club, 1909-10 season.

Knowle Rugby Football Club, 1919-20.

Knowle AFC, 1908-09 season.

Totterdown Athletic, late 1930s. Second from the left, at the back, is Harold Weeks and in the front row, second from the left, is his brother Ron. Totterdown Athletic was founded by the owner of the Knowle Cinema, Alderman Chamberlain.

Totterdown Athletic in 1948. Stan Bevan and Bill Hodge are at the back with Percy Hutching, Curly Blackman and George Nation in the front.

The opening of Perret's Park in 1932 by Councillor Perrett, who donated the land.

Celebrations of the coronation of King George VI in Highgrove Street, Totterdown, 1937.

Celebrating the coronation of Queen Elizabeth II in Jubilee Road, Knowle, 1953.

When all else fails to entertain there is always somebody else's misfortune to view. A slight mishap on Stanley Hill, Totterdown, 1968.

Nine

Wartime

The Second World War made a considerable impression on Knowle and Totterdown, which were heavily populated by the outbreak of hostilities in 1939. The concept of total war touched the life of the entire community. Many men were called to arms; women were pressed into work for the war effort and took the jobs vacated by those men in the forces, thus breaking new ground. Children were evacuated to rural areas. The hostilities were brutally brought home during the second half of 1940 by German air-raids on British cities. Bristol, as a major manufacturing centre and port, was a prime target and suffered a number of serious air attacks from 1940 to 1943. The proximity of Totterdown and Knowle to the railway lines, marshalling yards and main station caused many properties, homes, businesses, churches and other public buildings to be damaged or destroyed during bombing. There were consequently a number of fatalities and injuries. Life was also disturbed by false alarms, the black out and unexploded bombs. To protect the population, there were anti-aircraft units, air-raid wardens and the Home Guard, as well as the emergency services.

Exercise at the Three Lamps junction in early 1940. Mr Arthur Beavan is the fire-watcher in the white hat.

The Home Guard at Broad Walk in the early 1940s.

The Home Guard on Knowle cricket ground.

The warden's post at Wells Road School, 1941.

A German bomb – 'Titan' – weighing 1,800 kilograms. It was removed from outside No. 7 Beckington Road, Knowle in 1943, having been dropped on 14 April 1941.

A wartime wedding. Notice the blast protection on the windows.

Clyde Road, VE Day street party, 8 May 1945, with young and old alike enjoying the celebrations.

Outside No. 106 Crossways Road, Knowle, on VE night.

Queensdale Crescent, VE night.

Ten

Knowle

Development of a Suburb

Unlike near-by Brislington, Knowle seems to have missed out as regards the building of substantial houses. The fragment of Sir John Inyn's house at Inns Court, and the sixteenth-century Clancy's Farm are all that remains from only a small number of large properties.

Large houses such as Knowle House and Firfield House, were demolished for private building developments. Farms such as Queensdale disappeared for the building of council estates.

As early as 1917, it was realised that there was a shortage of some 5,000 houses in Bristol if the existing poor conditions were to be alleviated and 'homes fit for heroes' provided. Village suburbs were planned using a 75 per cent government contribution and built at St John's Lane and Knowle Park. In 1920, 130 acres of land were purchased from the Smyth estate for £40,500 and Knowle Park then was then laid out to provide homes for the better off council tenants under the 1919 Housing Act. Knowle Park was built to very high standards – 12 houses to the acre – the roads, e.g. Broad Walk, having verges and trees.

The Neville Chamberlain Act gave the council chance to clear poor properties in the Dings and St Philips and further housing was built at Knowle to house the people displaced. However, government subsidy was cut and the houses built e.g. Throgmorton Road were of a lower standard with more to the acre.

As one travels further west to Filwood Park the standard again falls. The houses were built as homes for those removed from overcrowded areas of central Bristol. By 1939, about 27,600 people lived on the Knowle and Bedminster estates, but amenities did not keep up with the growth of the population – hence the number of roundsmen who flourished. In general, the residents had to travel to Bedminster or Totterdown and Knowle for their shopping and entertainment.

After the Second World War a large number of aluminium prefabricated houses were built at Inns Court and along Airport Road. They were replaced by permanent housing only in the 1970s.

The remaining fragment of Sir John Inyn's fifteenth-century fortified house. This is now surrounded by houses on the Novers Park estate.

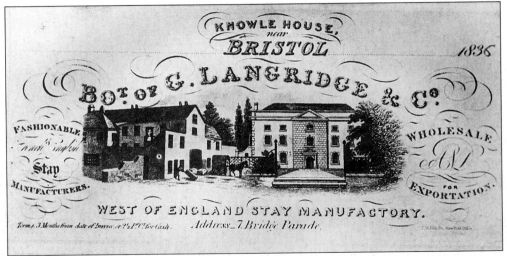

Knowle House, which was situated at the top of Talbot Hill on Priory Road. The façade appears to date from the early or mid-eighteenth century, but this could be a new frontage to a much older building. In 1836, it was owned by Langridges who made stays for corsets and who later moved to Avoncliff House on the Bath Road [see photograph on p 19]. Later, in 1895, Knowle House became the home of Alderman Frank Moore. It was a sad loss to Knowle when it was demolished.

Firfield House was built for John Hare, founder of Zion chapel in Bedminster, in the 1840s. It stood opposite The George public house on the Wells Road, and was demolished for the building of Belluton Road. The Hare family later owned the floorcloth, paint, varnish and linoleum works of Temple Meads and was a large employer of local labour. The family also had associations with Joseph Cottle who published the books of Wordsworth, Southey and Coleridge. This scene from 1893 shows Crimean War veterans being entertained by Alderman and Mrs Thatcher.

A view of Knowle and Knowle Park about 1933 looking towards Knowle West in the distance (the gas-holder is in Marksbury Road). In the foreground are the allotments of Talbot Hill. The Wells Road strikes across the centre of the picture, with the Red Lion Hill to the left. The pavilion to the Imperial Sports ground is in the left foreground. The Knowle estate has yet to be completed -Ilminster Avenue appears as a small unbuilt road to the left centre. Merrywood Boys' School will later occupy the large open area in the centre of the picture and Redcatch Park is yet to replace the allotments on the right.

Airport Road during construction. This rural scene is now much changed – all the trees have disappeared and the road has been greatly widened. This view is from the Wells Road looking towards Cadogan Road, with the houses to Ponsford Road off right.

Part of the workforce who built the roads in the Knowle area in the late 1920s and early 1930s. It is said that the number of the roads given Irish names was due to there being an Irish foreman on the building team; a large number of Irish families were also moved into the area.

Wellgarth Walk, Knowle. These were some of the earliest houses built in Knowle under the 1919 Housing Act and date from 1921-22. The picture shows the houses finished although the road is still unmade.

Broad Walk from Wells Road looking towards Axbridge Road. This shows the fine lay-out of the earliest estate, built in the early 1920s, with a wide road with verges and trees. The view was taken around 1933 when the houses built in Broad Walk were extended away from the Wells Road. Off right of this picture is the entrance to Redcatch Park and where the 'metal houses' were situated.

61-63 Broad Walk. These houses were the only two steel houses of this kind in Knowle. They were built in 1926 and are called Atholl houses. They were constructed of very large steel panels bolted together. The window frames were also huge steel sections bolted to the panels and reminiscent of portholes in a ship. It is said that the houses were prefabricated in the shipyards and were an attempt at building houses more cheaply. They were demolished in 1988.

Knowle Park, looking towards the Wells Road, with Brislington in the distance, *c.* 1935, clearly showing the well-planned and laid out streets of this early garden suburb. To the left are allotments between Broad Walk and Redcatch Road; Stoneleigh Road and Stoneleigh Crescent are yet to be built.

Glyn Vale and Lurgan Walk, 1933. These houses were erected to house families from the clearance areas in central Bristol, and appear spotless and new. Only one car is visible, but the area does seem well served by roundsmen – one selling milk from a motor-cycle and sidecar, another possibly a rag and bone man.

Novers Park, Inns Court and Knowle West, looking towards Knowle. Much of this area was built when Filwood Farm was demolished. Whitchurch Airport is just off the right of the picture. 425 homes were built at Inns Court to replace the temporary prefabricated dwellings that lined Airport Road. On the left can be seen Merrywood Girls' School which burnt down in August 1996.

Redcatch Road looking towards Wells Road, c. 1928. On the right are the allotments before the laying-out of Redcatch Park.

A very rural scene, but this was Redcatch Road around 1890, and is a reminder of the farming lifestyle which the building of Knowle totally displaced.

Eleven

Totterdown

A Suburb Destroyed

The first real housing development at Totterdown was after the building of the new Bath Road in 1833 [pp 23-24]. Totterdown was sparsely populated at this time, but this was to change with the coming of the railways in the 1840s. The proximity of Temple Meads railway station demanded a workforce nearby in those days before public transport.

The slopes of Pylle Hill were gradually built on from the middle of the last century, with house building snowballing in the 1860s and '70s. By the early 1880s, most of the green field sites had been built over, but further development was made possible by the demolition of Highgrove House. This building was situated at the end of Cemetery Road and its removal allowed the building of Balmain and Hawthorne streets. The house was once the home of Alfred Smith, ship-owner and coal-merchant, who became Lord Mayor of Bristol in 1905. Just before demolition, it was owned by Thomas Clarke, rope and twine manufacturer, who employed 37 men and boys.

Housing in Totterdown entered a long period of quiescence from the end of the last century until the 1960s. However, in 1967, an enquiry was held concerning a new multi-million pound outer circuit ring-road. The building of this scheme at Totterdown would necessitate the demolition of some 400 Victorian houses and 40 shops, mainly between the Bath and Wells Road.

It was programmed to start in 1972 when the first 120 properties were placed under compulsory purchase orders. However, although all the properties were gradually demolished, laying bare much of the hillside, no road development took place until the 1980s – and then only a watered-down scheme widening the two main roads. Fortunately, the cleared area has now been redeveloped and a new community born.

Lavars painting, 1887 – a detail of Totterdown showing its proximity to Temple Meads railway station and most of the houses built on Pylle Hill, except St Luke's Crescent, which as it was the steepest slope was left to last to develop.

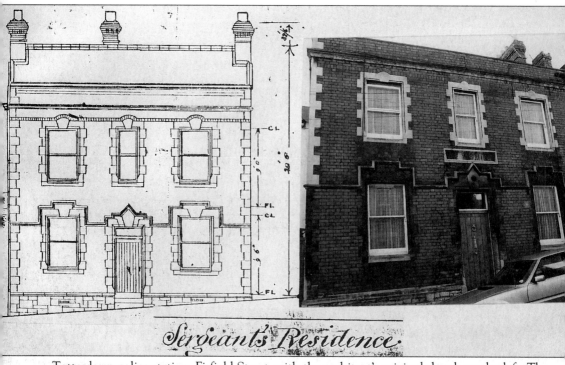

Sergeant's Residence.

Totterdown police station, Firfield Street, with the architect's original sketch on the left. The police station was built in 1882, by Charles King of Bitton, probably as the result of the recent growth of new housing in Totterdown and Knowle. The existing Bedminster and Bridewell stations were too distant to cover this new population. It cost the Justices of the Peace a princely sum of £637 plus the cost of the land purchased from a Mr H.J. Summers (who gave his name to the near-by Summers Hill). The original specification required a residence for a sergeant and with two cells attached; these are still in existence as part of a now private residence. The building was to be fitted with three flushing water-closet pans – one for each prisoner and one for the resident sergeant, at a cost of thirty-five shillings each – a luxury not many of the surrounding houses enjoyed. The original front door is still used, and was specified to be of two inches thick deal, with a strong mortice lock and two barrel bolts. The cell doors similarly were to be two inches thick but these were also be covered with thin sheet iron, and provided with a servery hatch ('at a cost of 30 shillings for each door – more or less'). The police station was not popular with the officers in charge as the site was seen to be inconvenient with a troublesome prisoner. The building was sold in 1898 for £805, after much haggling and later the new larger police station in Calcott Road, Knowle was constructed, which is also still in existence.

Upper St John's Lane. This small terrace of houses between the Wells Road and St Luke's Road were condemned as unfit as early as 1937, but demolished much later. The large house on the hillside top right is Bushy Lodge in Bushy Park.

This short terrace of five houses – Park Cottages – was situated behind Holy Nativity church and was cleared c. 1968. They were very tiny being only 10-feet wide and two up, two down. The park now occupies this site.

Kingstree Street in 1972. This short street ran between County Street and Angers Road and off left can be seen the entrance to Kingstree Terrace – a little backwater of six houses. New Walls Road is partially cleared in the distance.

New Walls Road in 1972, some of the houses typical of those cleared away for the road scheme.

The junction of New Walls Road and Bath Road in 1972. One must not forget the large variety and character of the houses demolished.

An aerial view of Pylle Hill 1972 [compare with p 123]. Clearance of houses has taken place around the periphery.

The cleared area of Totterdown – Oxford Street, New Walls Road, Angers Road, County Street, Highgrove Street and Bush Street as well as the Bath and Wells roads.

A model of the road scheme that was never built but for which the destruction of a close-knit community took place.